The Bullfrog
Does Not Imagine
New Towns

Bernard Jankowski

Washington Writers' Publishing House
Washington, D.C.

for Kate

Grateful acknowledgment is made to the following
publications in which some of these poems appeared:

*Baltimore Review, Cumberland Poetry Review, G.W. Review,
Monocacy Valley Review, Poet Lore, Poetry Daily, Potomac
Review, Sycamore Review, Visions-International, Willow Review,
WordWrights!*

Special thanks to manuscript editors Mary Ann Larkin and
Sid Gold of WWPH. Friendly thanks go to Steven Dobbin,
Michelle Flynn, Karen Gonya-Nickles, Bibi Graham-Reed,
and Patric Pepper for suggestions and encouragement.

Publication of this book is possible thanks to donations from
the many Friends of Washington Writers' Publishing House.

Cover and section break photographs of clock from former
Shamokin Silk Mill by A. Rick Harner, Carriage House
Studio, Shamokin, Pa.

Cover design by Lynn Springer/DL Graphics Studio.

Back cover photograph of Bernard Jankowski by Kathy
Jankowski.

Library of Congress Cataloging-in-Publication Data

Jankowski, Bernard, 1958-
    The Bullfrog Does Not Imagine New Towns / Bernard
Jankowski
    ISBN 0-931846-02-5 (alk. paper)
    I. Title.
PS3610.A37 B85 2001
811'.6--dc21

                                                    2001035966

WASHINGTON WRITERS' PUBLISHING HOUSE
P.O. Box 15271 Washington, D.C. 20003

I

Shamokin Graveyard   3
By the Seventh Bar   4
Buzzards   6
Old Women of Shamokin   7
Driving Aunt Rita to the Sanitarium   8
Gather in the Crows   9
The Source   10
Seven Shrunken Skulls   12
Mt. Carmel 1965   14
Fast Eddie   15

II

Apology to Vallejo   19
The City Never Leaves Us   21
Rita on Speedway Boulevard   22
Stuck Behind a Hearse   24
Dead Woman's Brandy   26
I Remember D.C. Raining   28
Pay Phone at the Bottom of Rock Creek   29
You Died Tonight in Wilmington   30
Blue Dogs   31
Shadow Boxer   33

III

The Bullfrog Does Not Imagine New Towns   37
The Silence Beyond the Carnival Grounds   38
Crickets   40
I Look for You, Frankie   41
Atlantic City Moon   42
Atlantic City Dawn   43
The Widow of Kill Devil Hills   45
Hatteras   46
Sonora, You Bring Me Nothing But Trouble   47
The Band That Played for One of My Deaths   49

IV

I Wander the Plazas for Trouble   53
Wanchese Harbor, 2 a.m.   54
A Man in Love With a Woman Who Is 33 Women   56
Honeymoon in Harpers Ferry   58
Your Wife Is up a Tree   59
This Skin   60
Poem Inspired by Love Paintings at the American
    Visionary Art Museum   62
The Wish   65
Junkyard   66
Song to the Potomac   67

Shamokin Graveyard

Bored with these years etched and rotting,
pumpkin-headed babies ice-skate
among the plastic bouquets.

Sulphur rises from mounds of culm,
smokes through snow and bluster — coal dust
ribbons through the streets.

On the hillside, the blanched-out birch trees
stand like miners' arms
resting from the black and blue.

In my grave,
a long line of large-hipped women
plod the creaking wooden stairs
to sleep.

By the Seventh Bar

You think this town looks mean by day,
with its coal-sooted storefronts,
men cut hard in their 50s hats,
women who chip away
at each other over a Woolworth's lunch?

Tonight, with a moon shot
over the mounds of culm,
this town rides its coal-hard soul
deep into the night.

The guy on the jukebox
lost his wife and
another has no wife,
and the guy sitting next to you
offers you his wife.

You've managed to make friends with
the only deaf-mute in town
and you swap buying beers
until he's broke and
you end up buying all night.

He follows you and your cousin
from bar to bar, a character
out of the Brothers Grimm.

He stands
in the middle of the street.
The moral of the story
is in his head.
He taps his temples
with his forefingers,
snaps his skull around.
He wants to let it loose,
but can't, so he smiles sweetly
and points to another bar.

By the seventh bar, you run
into guys named Black.
Jack Black, Black Bart, Black Heart,
nicknames like tattoos.
Tonight it's Black Hawk —
a Pittsburgh-born, truck driving,
retread Hippie, quarter-Indian hard ass.

Black Hawk, in a somber drunk,
wants to show you his kids
in his wallet, to be tender.
Your cousin is playing the wise guy,
saying "You don't know your kids.
All you got is a wallet full of kids."

By the seventh bar, it's time
to burn off some of this evil.
You stare back at the bar and
your cousin feels
Black Hawk's fist coming down.

Seven bars: The Hard Shell, Hawk's Nest, Polish Home,
Par Three, Garden Club, Janie's, and the Brass Rail.

You live the story like your uncles —
someone has to carry on this bad blood.

Buzzards

Up in the shadows,
dark leaves twitch
and grumble.

Twelve dark buzzards,
twelve dark priests,
betray my confessions
and grin
at tales of my foolishness.

Old Women of Shamokin

December has her own
caverns for the sun.
A bitter wind rustles
down the aisles.
Blank brown sunflower
faces stare, silent.

These ladies last one more winter —
shoulders stooped deep
inside their coats.
Using only tiny canes,
swollen ankles manage
the night ice.

Once, they made sunflower faces
and swayed with the sun,
jumping rope,
their heads
filled with light.

Now, time sends solitary
blue wolves wandering
through their eyes.

At St. Stanislaus, the women gather.
The shrill wail of "Ave Maria"
purges the blood,
then sails off
beyond the peaks of coal.

Out in the fields,
stalks mumble rosaries
beneath another snow.

Driving Aunt Rita to the Sanitarium

My father and I wait
in the alley
in the long blue Buick
as my Mom and Aunt Miriam
carefully escort
Aunt Rita down the fire escape.

I'm only 10,
dressed in my Sunday best,
wedged between two aunts,
disoriented by the glint
of October sunshine,
the strange crinkly warmth
of polyester,
the intoxication of starch,
sweet perfumes,
Miriam's chittery laugh, and
our final destination:

The Sanitarium, a far-off,
never-seen, antiseptic place,
serene and quiet,
maybe even holy.

Up front, my parents'
make-talk
drops like tiny lost keys
into the darkness
that surrounds Rita.

We silently huddle
as the long blue Buick drifts
through the Sanitarium gates.
Rita sits straight and stiff,
her cold hand gripping mine,
her lipstick drawn
in a sad, sweet smile
over her mouth,
which ticks.

Gather in the Crows

Gather in the crows
you cut out as a child.

Allow these fields of rotted pumpkins
to swell. On this cliff-edge

your head is clanking with drunken uncles
smoking cigars, ready to ride.

Below, the white bellies of catfish
roll like moons through luminous mud.

Wrapped in each November oak, a monk
prays for your delivery.

The Source

The stirring
was coming on again,
his memory of being

abandoned in a nest of eaglets,
then stolen by crows

and tossed off

tumbling

like a riddle
into the wide brown Potomac. . . .

only to be washed up on a beach
below Great Falls,

nursed to health
by a copperhead

spinning its alchemy
of diamonds and pain.

This restlessness
that searches
for the bold innocence

of birth in the sweet-salt muscle
of a Norfolk shipyard,

hardens and blackens
on the tiles
of a Baltimore bus station,

itches beneath his
business-world shirt,

rolls across his
dreaming wife's back,

trudges
over strip-mined Appalachian hills,

and ends up on the river bank,
searching for a past, a song.

Seven Shrunken Skulls

It is getting late,
real late,
when the dead buck mounted
behind the bar
asks me questions
and I feel I have to respond.

It is getting late,
when I stare
into the buck's
marble eyes and
conjure up images
from the lives
of my cousins.

Roaming bars, pool rooms, and racetracks,
losing the rent at blackjack,
botching robberies, punching cops,
mocking judges, gutting families.

And in the end, waits
the state of ungrace.
Found alone, bloated
from booze or death
in a mountain cabin.
Half-faced, fallen
next to a rifle
in a rented room.
Shipwrecked in a T-Bird
at the bottom of a ravine.

If my cousins were here,
they would charm me
with another drink,
swing me into a good time,
persuade me to spin
a few more hours
down that hole.

12

I leave the bar alone.
That dead buck's off my back,
but my cousins' seven
shrunken skulls are strung
around my neck.

As I walk away,
the skulls start to click
and jangle.
Up the street,
another bar's
neon blinks, "Drinks."

Mt. Carmel 1965

My Aunt Martha and NoNo
sit in the kitchen
without the lights on,
in the twilight
of the coal town's sleepy day.

They speak their Old Country tongue.
The comfort in their words blends
with the smell of butter-browned
gnocchi that drifts into the yard,
where I kick a flattened,
coal-dusted ball
against an abandoned garage.

This memory remains
not in the logic
or the letters
or the words.

This memory
is of the sounds
we made,
as a certain light
fell around us.

Fast Eddie

You tell the one again
about the midget
lifting a refrigerator,
the one-armed drywaller
from Highlandtown,
and the crooked
Baltimore City cop.
But it doesn't get
the same guffaws.

You still try to
rise like a hero
for the sunup to
sundown suckers,
beat your chest once more
at the whorehouses,
rattle the monkeys
in their cages.
But you've overheard
from the regulars,
"Eddie's gettin' pathetic."

It was never on the map
for you to change.
Each Saturday night
like the hundreds before it:
Comb Baltimore for a Hotspot
ready to get hotter.
Chase the Fells Point waitresses,
"those heavenly little oven-stuffers."
Hang with men
who don't mind
a bullet in the thigh.
Leave everyone to wonder
what your next move will be.

Catch a few hours sleep and
then roar into another Sunday:
Make the Pimlico
backstretch your stage
and the jockeys your stooges.
Pop a cannonball
with your suit on
into a pool filled with nieces.
Leave your family frightened
to invite you to weddings.

By now, it's getting old.
Your settled-down friends
won't return your calls.
You work your way down
your list of run-around friends,
past the ones who
are dead or married,
past the guys who
were divorced for awhile
but then got remarried,
down to the guys who
really don't like to drink or
who don't like to talk.

Until you realize,
"Hey, my nephews
are old enough now."
You grin to yourself,
it sounds like a plan,
"Nephews."

II

Apology to Vallejo

Dear Vallejo,
I apologize for I have
died so little today.

I blindly strode past
the clenched hands
at the bus stop
dissolving in the rain,
watched the beggars raid
their baskets
without my prayers,
failed to face
the trains' icy breezes,
as they rushed by
with their heavy loads
of mannequins and masks
and occasionally a child.

Vallejo, dear Vallejo,
how I ignored
the secretaries diligently
typing into blue infinity,
the pigeons clinging to tiny hopes
on the telephone wires,
the slick black umbrellas
protecting the commuters
like shells.

I was not up
to your grim commitment.
I had nothing left for
the dentists — so many teeth!
the housewives — so many chickens!
for the mid-level managers,
the gas station attendants,
the cooks, the dry cleaners,
the priests.

The city surrounded me.
So many deaths to die!
And I spent all day
absorbed in my own.

The City Never Leaves Us

— for Sid Gold

Nickel-eyed pigeons
in business gray pluck crackers
while schizoid hobos
sleeptalk the news.

This city is our city —
Mayan-masked bums
chew lunches
of fetid cheese,
Vietnam vets battle traffic
with toothbrushes,
winos rot
beneath the elms.

There is always "the waiting."
We are waiting
for gunfire or a messenger
to honk and hand us
a new pet or new lives.

We take kindly to statues,
sweeping their feet,
reading them the papers.
We spend twilights
scrubbing graffiti
from their breasts
and pigeon-shit
from their proud hair.

We grow old,
go to older movies.
We have each other
but need more —
filling the days with
dark bread and dark jokes.

The city never leaves us.
So we sleep,
as bronzed buffaloes
graze on air
and the hour is repaved.

Rita on Speedway Boulevard

Rita, you stood by the boulevard
in the blinding mid-day Tucson light
as traffic rushed by,
sweat beading on your forehead,
dark curls wigged out,
glasses askew,
shopping bags bursting
their bottoms.

You were 23, olive-skinned,
Boticelli-beautiful.
Who would ever know?
It was always a bit too much
to pull together.

The tractor-trailers belched and
the beat pickups smoked.
A delirious strip
of eye-level haze was
just right to bend your mind.
You looked ready to trip, Rita,
right into the traffic,
to spill your bags, faint.
You needed someone
to take you by the hand.

You didn't see me wave to you
through all that chaos.
I was late for work and
couldn't turn around and
give you a ride.
I guess you caught a bus.

I moved back East
a few weeks later.
Never saw you again,
that was 12 years ago.
It worries me,
from time to time,
what became of you, Rita.
I'm not entirely sure
you ever made it home.

Stuck Behind a Hearse

Stuck behind a hearse,
for once I didn't succumb
to the inner monologue
pushing "c'mon, c'mon."
Didn't shuffle through
the rolodex in my mind
to see who I would disappoint
or annoy by being late.
I just let it go,
decided to accept
the hearse for what it was —

a black reminder
that rode long
and cool and clean.
I settled in behind it
and took in the day
like I never do.
Took in the day
like I had all
the time in the world.

I couldn't make out
the hearse driver's face.
I assumed it was set in stone,
with a five-o'clock shadow,
a few flecks of red in his eyes,
an unflappable face
like most of the pros
who get their paychecks from death.

I envied the patience
that driver held
beneath his black hat,
the serenity
of his crisp black
slow-driving world.

The hearse's wake calmed
everything down to slow-motion.
I watched the late October
shadows of crows
drift by on the pavement,
felt the stoic clock
poised inside my blood.

Dead Woman's Brandy

When you die, your brandy
will end up in an alley,
drunk up by three borrachos
beneath the sleeping offices.

— *Corrida for a Dead Woman*
by Oscar and Carlos

I never even met you,
but was volunteered by my wife
to empty your house for the friend
of a friend of a friend.
I wasn't happy about it,
complained, was "insensitive,"
called you "that dead lady."

Each time the mourners
brought out another picture
of you in Cleveland
or Cancun, I tried not to
remember your face.

I carried your possessions
to this alley with two Mexicans.
If this is a note to you, then
their names are Oscar and Carlos.
Good men — we moved your
things swiftly past
the ever-changing group
of grievers.

My friend, Mo, a dry cleaner,
said I could lose your stuff
in the dumpster behind
his store. The night watchman
barked at us, so I bribed him
with a half-full bottle
of your cognac.

Somehow, I ended up
at the end of your line.
We threw out your belongings.
Drank up all your brandy.

I'm left
with your empty
wooden chest, now filled
with my son's toys,
a fuzzy head from your
too-sweet liqueurs, and
a secret:

When we moved your bed,
I grabbed hold of the box-frame —
the thin skin of cloth ripped and
for a moment
I held your rib.

I Remember D.C. Raining

How some mornings
I would wake
and look out
our basement apartment window
and see 8th Street
leaden with rain.
WPFW would be playing
Mingus or Mose Allison
and Georgia Avenue
was waiting
for me to pace
the sidewalks,
feel the raincoated silence
of the others,
catch a blurry glimpse
of my eye in a puddle,
hear the weary honks
of the beat-up taxis and
the whoosh of their retreads,
pass the streaks of rain
on the vacant storefront windows,
as solitude
stepped out
of a boarded-up rowhouse
to greet me.

Pay Phone at the Bottom of Rock Creek

It is good to find a pay phone
at the bottom of Rock Creek —
watch the water
silently drown out
the drivel of D.C.,
let the worn-out words sleep.

I don't want to think about
the melodrama that brought
that phone to this creek —
the screaming lover that
tore it from the booth,
the hoodlums and vandals,
the vicious drug dealers and pimps,
the paranoid jerks, the whores —
the deal-makers, deal-breakers,
the big-timers — enough.
Let it rest.

Silence brings
a murmur of minnows
up to the receiver.

The phone rusts
in the sweet creek's
shifting sands.

This is my news tonight.

You Died Tonight in Wilmington

— for Matt O'Neill (1961-2000)

You died tonight in Wilmington,
too young,

like you always did,

when it snowed
and you lay your lips to vodka,

like you always would,

in Wilmington,
when it snows

and a train shoves off
hunting with yellow night eyes

and whoooo-whooooooes
into the bluster,

like it always does,

sweeping over the snow
like a big black owl.

Blue Dogs

We are left
with what you have left us:
slavering tongues,
ribs strapped with skin,
our flea-bitten hides and
corkscrew eyes — We run
in the knocked-out,
storm-blue light.

When you see our seedy pack
startled and exposed,
don't stare too long,
don't press your luck,
just get on home.
We have dragged down
many a gawking parlor boy.

Our chains to the moon and
the shine of our steely distance
keep the homebodies at bay.
We ride hungers
deeper than
your warm hearth.
There is always
another dream.

We shed hard darkness
into the first slivers of sun.
While you sleep, we roam
your grand plazas, mock
your pigeon-strewn gods, forage
in the trashcan luxury
of the moon.

Rest well among
your fellow citizens.
If you have a nightmare,
turn on your light.
You will never wake
to this darkness:

We do what we wish
in our half
of your world.

Shadow Boxer

Shadows jut
from the walls,
taunting his hands
with their jabs —
hands that could smash
this radio, break through
these studs, dismantle
a man.

He imagines his flesh
ringing in silks,
rising above the crowds —
his path of destruction
legit and resolute.
He will leave them
bellowing his name.

These shadows of bosses,
women's names,
strange towns,
they fall with the night —
he brings his fists
and an uneven mind
to the gathering smoke.

He dances this violence,
past bouts storm
in his wake —
shadow-flesh and
shadow-heart battle
the shifting,
bobbing forms.

Once-rocked,
twice-rocked . . . . all night,
the images flicker —

each opponent dissolves
down an echoing hall.

III

The Bullfrog Does Not Imagine New Towns

The bullfrog
does not imagine
new towns or cling
to wispy dreams.

The bullfrog
lays its soft belly
on the wet belly
of the swamp
and emanates
the night's
first tantric croak.

Others soon
join in, together,
they gain strength —

All night, the bullfrogs
dig deep down
into the mud
and free
the dark song
of the swamp's
grieving throat.

The Silence Beyond the Carnival Grounds

The silence
beyond the carnival grounds
threatens,
it threatens the little boy
who has school tomorrow,
it threatens the grownups
who will return to their jobs,
the carny manning
the spinning teacups,
Helga the Hermaphrodite
in his/her dressing room,
the sword swallower,
and the jabbering
Ginzu salesman, too.

It waits, lurks.
The silence
where mirrors don't make
your head six feet tall,
where the clown who berates you
is yelling through his closed car window,
where you can't take a Ferris wheel
high above it all.

The Carnival Owner knows
the silence.
He's moved from town to town
for 40 years now.
The alcoholic albino Snakekeeper
knows it.
The teenage runaway Age-and-Weight Guesser
knows it.
The Harley guy with the skull and snake tattoos
running the baby rides
knows it, and
the obnoxious Drown the Clown guy
knows it, too.

Tonight, as the midway shuts down,
the transformers stop roaring,
and the carnies
down their last beer,
the Smallest Woman in the World
lies on her tiny cot
in her tiny house,
ignoring the buzz
on her black and white TV,
and wonders
if maybe the silence
is a way
to some other side.

Crickets

Wake to a whistle-stop,
the crickets are singing.
This long, black train unravels
long, black threads of Louise
humming in her slip.

Framed by the fading tracks,
you see her finger
draw that line in the air —
"That's it. You just crossed it."

Outside, the song stretches
clear across Kansas.
Is that Louise in the night
or the crickets?

I Look for You, Frankie

I look for you, Francis Ignatius,
not half-jaded, half-gone
like you were in college.
The Frankie everyone knew
before you married
the police captain's lost little girl,
that hooker from The Block,
or lost your kids and her from
too much his-and-hers cocaine.

I look for you, Frankie,
but you're phoneless again,
probably carless.
I imagine you
as you might be tonight,
sweating the August darkness away
in some Fells Point kitchen,
door open to the alley,
Pall Mall dangling,
bemused or befuddled or bored
by another steaming pot
of writhing blue crabs.

Atlantic City Moon

Lonely figures
pace the boardwalk
like props in
a DeChirico streetscape.
They wonder,
how did it happen?
All that money, gone,
and I wonder about you,
Moon, and how you
pull me away
with your full,
ripe tides.

Play that song
by the Drifters.
I want to lure
the luscious moon
beneath the boardwalk
into the darkness
and wet sand
and roll with her
among the paper cups
and newsprint.

I want to let it ride
with you, Moon,
to roll with you.
But I see you've been
bought, and you're painted
and for sale and
stuffed with silver coins.

I don't have
the right lines,
the right clothes,
or the hundred bucks.

Atlantic City is no town
for a man to
wish innocence
upon the moon.

Atlantic City Dawn

You recall the night before
with its busloads
of over-eager seniors
evaporating like mist
into the Gotham
of casinos
and the relentless
crescendo of slots.

How the dice
anxiously clicked —
eyes grew wide
until they blinked
and the exquisite
croupier focused
on his new prey.

Black jacks snapped
on the green felt,
while players searched
for compassion
and a soft hit
in the dead-eyed
glare of the dealer.

Chips swelled
with childish hope,
only to be reclaimed,
justifying the cold
calculations
of the anonymous
men upstairs.

On the beach,
loaders struggle
around the clock
to build up the shore,
while the sea
rips it back
again and again.

Up and down
the boardwalk,
empty-pocketed mutterers
hold courtesy
cups of coffee
in jittery hands,
not yet ready
to admit defeat
to the meager dawn.

The Widow of Kill Devil Hills

Wounds streak
the Hatteras sky.
A never-ending wind chases
the shifting dunes
while the jukebox drags
the tradesmen
through another night.

The sea pounds
the shore into darkness.
Carpenters bitch and drink.
The widow waits,
three blocks away.

The widow whistles
through the men's empty bottles,
mocks their wives, slips
into their dreams.

There's a hunger
behind the jukebox, a hunger
behind the men's dimes —
the widow wind
becomes the song.

Sunday morning is wounded.
A woman wakes to find
her husband's back torn
by the widow's red etch.

She runs from their shack
across the dunes. Howls
into the widow wind.
It whistles in return.

Her husband twists
in the mirror
and shudders,
as he fingers
the lightning bolt
streaked across his back.

45

Hatteras

Down there,
the March wind
is constant.

It wakes you
with a stiff chill
that pricks the skin
beneath your stubble,
reddens your forearms
as you bang
your daily nails,
whips sand
against your teeth
when you grit
back at the boss.
You turn, it's there,
that wind,
following you
like a hound.

The wind swirls
the ice cubes
of your last
rum and coke,
shoves you home,
rattles the shutters
of your shack,
paces and wails
outside the door
like a death hound,
searching for a seam,
a crack, a way
to keep at you.

Sonora, You Bring Me Nothing But Trouble

Sonora, you bring me
nothing but trouble,
yet you ride beside me
in my pickup,
stars smiling like
the first necklace
ripped from the earth.

I know why he
wants to keep you — you sing
and tin trumpets
call up the moon — cry
and tequila licks
upon our wounds — laugh
and the mariachis call
the slumbering marionettes
to dance.

You bring all your night
upon me, Sonora,
and I have nothing left.

You know by now
the old boy is waking,
eyes trembling on
an empty nest.
He will rage for his bride
and bring on his light
and we will scurry
like roaches for the border.

Is Hermosillo north or south of here?
There are not enough roads.
What will I tell the folks back home?

I have stolen the rooster's bride!
I have stolen the rooster's bride!

You bring me nothing
but trouble, Sonora —
You with your nights
and him with his days.

The Band That Played for One of My Deaths

The alto sax player
used to blow with James Brown,
but then drank too much.

The tenor sax man
is a stone mason during the day —
his body, arms, and fingers
never fit the instrument.

The organist was a white-boy
who wanted to be black,
and was wasting
everybody's time.

The trumpet player
was from Mexico.
He stood straight-up,
mariachi-style,
and struggled with "the jazz."

The bass player
didn't show up.

The lead guitar was a guy
I'd never pay to hear.

The singer sang with
B.B. King on his way up.

The drummer was solid.

They knew I came
from the same
in-between world.

They knew we
were all headed
nowhere.

They knew it was time
to blow
or be blown.

Till 4 a.m.,
they played their hearts out.
Lovingly, they butchered
all my requests.

IV

I Wander the Plazas for Trouble

Since you have turned me loose,
I wander the plazas for trouble.

Comfort can come in low forms, indeed,
when a man is down on his knees.

Stone angels spew water and grin for a reply —
I blacken their eyes.

Rooftop gargoyles watch me, watch me —
I stuff pigeons down their throats.

This bum wants a buck and then another —
I scatter them with stones.

It has become very simple. I owe nothing
but all this time on my hands.

I retire at the feet of a Greek goddess.
Perhaps I will rest, perhaps rot.

Her eyes are set by casts, well-fired,
undreaming — like eyes all over town,

like yours
when you threw me out.

Wanchese Harbor, 2 a.m.

Flounder slap, ice-packed,
2 a.m. shipped.
Tractor-trailer lurches
from the dock,
jolting tired, creaking
dinosaur bones.

You are left
with the small-town glow
of the carnival lights
strung along the masts.

The lighthouse
blinks counterfeit.
The sleeping ship harbor,
a mirage.
Stars tossed about,
crap-shot jewelry —
they will not
lead you home.

Walk these
clatter-teethed planks.
Follow the wolves
that leap into mist.
Silent masks
of boarded-up arcades —
no song along the pier.

Four times tonight,
your cot
drifts out to sea.

Four times tonight,
the waves knead
bread for the dying.

Four times tonight,
her shape offers
you an hourglass.

Dream-scraps scurry
for their corners,
shutters twitch
against the shack,

you never told her goodbye.

A Man in Love with a Woman Who is 33 Women

A man in love
with a woman who is 33 women
is always chasing her around
or waiting for her to stop
or watching other men watch her
or drowning in her kaleidoscopes
or searching for some vague
scientific hope.

Don't examine the dichotomies,
"blessing or curse,"
"bitch or blessing."
She's 33 women
and the possibilities
are mind boggling.
So boggle your mind
or enjoy the swirl —
it's 33 women
you're dancing with,
33 women
you're talking with,
and it's a squabble
on the phone
with 33 women,
and you know
such a squabble
could never end.

Consider yourself her master,
her, your harem.
But it's a joke —
no king ruled 33 women,
no Casanova controlled 33 women.

She descends the staircase
in her 33 shades of Duchamp
and you are gone
down her 33 roads,
kissing her 66 lips,
and listening to her 33 tongues
to which you only have
the capability
of understanding
at the most three.
And you're fool enough,
now, to wonder,
how
she owns you
so.

Honeymoon in Harpers Ferry

Who are these dark angels
hovering over our bed?
Who sent them?
Why are they whispering?

Ancestors are scurrying
about our room.
Crows are gathering
on the windowsills.
Uncles are quarreling,
perched on the weathervane,
spinning on our roof.

They want to invade,
offer advice, incite.
They want to drop
rumors in our ears.
Ancestors know well
seeds are patient
and shortcomings
can take years
to sprout their
cold truths upon us.

The cliffs,
the clouds,
and the river
bring me to you.

Let me imagine,
high above
the Shenandoah and Potomac,
what life will be like
with you, without
their stone confidence
in the past.

Your Wife Is Up a Tree

Your wife is up a tree
and you can't get her down.

No pleading, no "sorrys,"
No "You're making too much of this."

She has made up her mind.

If you chopped the tree down,
she'd climb another.
If you set it on fire,
she'd die a martyr.

It has always been this way
with you and your kind,
ignorant Polish drunks
sending bawling women up trees.
What pleading! What brutes! What remorse!

She shape-shifts in her tree —
first the Virgin Mary,
then Guinevere,
then an elegant, white goose.

You want them all.
You want to call out to her,
to sing her down
with a memory.

But she's run out of shapes.
You call to her.
She's turning toward
the oak.

This Skin

Was this skin
waiting for you
like a tramp's bag
at the bus stop,
a potato sack
in the back
of a pickup,
a third-hand suit
at the Salvation Army?

This skin
is a frayed map.
Must have been
previously used,
sold, resold,
hired out,
tossed on a stoop,
flung on a train.
It feels like it's lived
elsewhere, traveled many places,
like an old spy's raincoat
or a crow's ragged frock.

Maybe it was fished
out of the Chesapeake
or stolen off a West Virginia nag —
it does tend to stray
toward rivers and pastures
and sometimes gets an odd itch
to graze.

Born so blue and bright
and right, it's nicked
and weathered, wrinkled
and brown,
and like a mopey dog,
it follows you through your days.

You drag it,
sometimes it drags you.
It's your passport
to another,
your vague and incessant
animal hope —

But how to get from here to there?

You think
you would know
each other
better by now.

Poem Inspired by Love Paintings
at the American Visionary Art Museum

There was a pattern

before time —
a hope,
a seed,
a gene,
a breeze —
burned into the skin,
the eye,
the brain.

A vision —
Beatrice,
Gauguin's exotics,
Grocery-line magazines.

Who could live up
to such expectations?

She would have to.

You stitched me

as your man,
a great man,
like some comic-book hero
or movie star.

I couldn't make
the grade, the costume
didn't fit.

I wilted from
the pattern
and drained
like gutter oil
into the harbor.

Worse, I melted
into the other men
you pass by
on the street.

I could not
overcome
or
unbe.

I stitched you

into my man's
whatta-woman-should-be
pattern. You burst.

Into my whore's pattern.
You burst.

Into my schoolmarm's pattern.
You burst and

you burst and then,
in your ultimate grace,
you said, "Here, baby,
put your fingers here."

It helps this pain

some
to define you
with my needles.

The barbs hurt,
I know,
but then
there's your silence.

Last night I slept

wrapped up
in your nylons.

It soothed me
to recreate
your shadows.

Then I woke
and twisted them.
I strangled the pillow
that's become
my mate.

The Wish

— for Steven Dobbin

The wish
was floundering
in a succession
of days.

The grass was green, green.
The sky was blue, blue.
The neighbors were perky, perky.
The children were clean, clean.

The wish
was like a tic
on the soul,
it was selfish,
it was dreamy,
it was a question,
it was sure.

The wish
imagined an alley,
or a troll's hole
beneath a bridge.
It whispered,
"Rim-baud, Rim-baud,
Bau-de-laire, Bau-de-laire."

In a succession
of days the same,
the wish
slept underground
like a snake, cool
as a diamond.

Years later,
the wish stirred.
Up above,
a neighbor was
whistling
and shoveling
mulch.

Junkyard

Why is beauty drawn
to demise?
Drawn to this rust,
with the wastrel wild
flowers blooming
between
the rotted
foam bucket seats.

Why is love
drawn to a Chevy?
And despair overcome
by the cool fins,
the aqua-blue panels,
and the AM radio
stuck
on stone-cold R&B.

Even if it all ends in rust,
it is wonderful to know
that for a time
it (the car) and we (the young lovers)
get to ride
down a road
we never imagine
will end.

Song to the Potomac

Before I walked the city dead and found this river bank,

before I asked the river again to soothe my memory,

before I had and lost Kate a dozen times,

before wine convinced me I should have been a herring,

before Spring mud renewed my faith in laziness,

before the ghosts of weary laborers appeared floating above
the river,

before my friends spilled secrets on the misty banks,

before fireflies blinked in the summer-loved grasses,

before bones of buried canal mules rattled for a rest,

before my love was freed by the songs of William Blake,

before Kate's Scottish skin blushed at 20 and 30 and now,

before I bumped into a copperhead while swimming,

before a catfish begged me to let it go,

before the carp's tail flopped in the August sun,

before the Canada goose mourned for his lost mate,

before the winter-white sycamore led me to my first death,

before angel paws of foxes escaped on the frozen canal,

before a Barred Owl turned to share Kate's sorrowful,
brown eyes.

Before all this, the river,
charged and muddy and deep,

flowed on like memory.